CW01238270

Original title:
Horizons Awakened by Joyful Dreams

Copyright © 2025 Swan Charm
All rights reserved.

Author: Aron Pilviste
ISBN HARDBACK: 978-9908-1-2917-4
ISBN PAPERBACK: 978-9908-1-2918-1
ISBN EBOOK: 978-9908-1-2919-8

In the Glow of Endless Possibilities

In the dawn's soft embrace, we rise,
With whispers of hope in the skies.
Each step unfolds a story anew,
In the glow, our dreams break through.

Paths untraveled call us near,
With every heartbeat, we persevere.
The light guides us, a gentle hand,
In this journey, together we stand.

Old fears fading, like shadows cast,
We forge ahead, unbound and vast.
With courage bright and spirits high,
In the glow of dreams, we learn to fly.

Beneath the stars, our wishes soar,
Each moment's magic, an open door.
Embracing change, we dance with fate,
In endless possibilities, we create.

So let us wander, explore, and seek,
For the heart is strong, and the soul is unique.
In the glow of life, we find our way,
Dreaming boldly, come what may.

Journeys Between Dreams and Light

In quiet hours when shadows merge,
We travel paths where fantasies surge.
Between the day and night's sweet kiss,
A world unfolds, a gentle bliss.

Through whispered tales, the stars inspire,
Guiding our hearts like a burning fire.
With every dream a breath taken,
A journey awaits, unshaken, unbroken.

We chase the dawn with hopeful eyes,
Embracing the truth beneath the skies.
Step by step, with spirits bright,
We weave our fate in soft twilight.

As daylight dims and shadows grow,
In the heart's embrace, our courage flows.
Journeys linger where dreams ignite,
Bathed in the magic of purest light.

Hand in hand, we'll wander wide,
Lost in a world where dreams abide.
In this dance of dreams and light,
Together we'll soar into the night.

The Sunlit Path to Tomorrow

Awash in gold, the edges gleam,
The sunlit path holds every dream.
With every step, the future calls,
Inviting hearts to rise and fall.

Each moment glistens, fresh and bright,
Drawing us close with pure delight.
The road ahead, with twists and turns,
Holds countless gifts for which we yearn.

In laughter shared or silent grace,
The sun's warm touch, a soft embrace.
Together we walk, no fear to borrow,
Into the light of a shining tomorrow.

With eyes that sparkle and spirits bold,
New stories waiting to be told.
The journey smiles, with open arms,
As sunlight dances, and hope warms.

So let us step into the glow,
Where all our wildest dreams can grow.
On the sunlit path, we find our way,
Towards the promise of a new day.

Boundless Dreams in the Dawnlight

At dawn's first breath, the sky ignites,
Unfolding dreams in vibrant sights.
The world awakens from soft slumber,
With whispers of hope, a joyous wonder.

As colors dance and shadows flee,
We find our way, you and me.
In each new moment, the heart expands,
Embracing life with open hands.

With courage found in morning's grace,
We follow paths we dare to trace.
The dawn invites, with golden rays,
To chase the dreams of endless days.

Boundless visions rise and shine,
In this sacred space, we intertwine.
Together, drawn by starlit schemes,
We nurture the fire of our dreams.

So let us wander, fearless and free,
In the dawnlight's magic, just you and me.
For every step leads further still,
Into a world where dreams fulfill.

Dawning Colors of Serendipity

In the early glow of day,
Colors dance and play away.
Each hue a story to unfold,
A canvas bright, a sight to behold.

The sun peeks through the misty veil,
Winds of change begin to sail.
Nature whispers, soft and sweet,
A symphony of joy, complete.

Morning light paints the trees,
Breezes hum with tranquil ease.
In this moment, hearts take flight,
Dawning dreams awaken bright.

Every shade holds a secret wish,
In gentle strokes, our souls refresh.
A world reborn with each soft ray,
Embracing hope, come what may.

As colors merge, a tale begins,
Of paths unworn and quiet wins.
The beauty found in what may be,
In dawning colors, we are free.

Whispers of Hope in the Morning Light

In the hush of dawn's embrace,
Hope ignites with tender grace.
Every beam a gentle nudge,
Awakens dreams, will not budge.

Stars fade softly, night's own sigh,
A promise made, to soar and fly.
Clouds recede in golden hues,
Spreading warmth, a heartfelt muse.

Morning dew upon the grass,
Sparkling bright as moments pass.
In quiet streets, the world awakes,
With every whisper, hope remakes.

Birds sing sweetly from the trees,
Carrying tales upon the breeze.
Painting skies with colors bold,
Stories of strength and dreams retold.

Each daybreak brings new delight,
In whispers soft, we find our light.
Embrace the dawn, let spirits rise,
In morning's glow, the heart complies.

Chasing Rainbows Beyond the Clouds

After the storm, when skies turn clear,
We seek the arcs that draw us near.
Colors burst in radiant hues,
A promise drawn, we shall not lose.

With every raindrop that cascades,
A melody of hope invades.
Footprints on the path so bright,
Guiding souls to the light.

Through silver linings, dreams take flight,
Chasing rainbows, pure delight.
A tapestry of tales untold,
In vibrant crafts, our hearts unfold.

The horizon holds a mystery,
Of endless skies and history.
Chasing dreams beyond the gray,
We find our joy in each new day.

As we reach for colors anew,
In every heart, a world to view.
Together we shall dance and sing,
Chasing rainbows, jubilee we bring.

The Symphony of a New Dawn

In dawn's embrace, a symphony,
Notes of life in harmony.
Whispers rise with every breeze,
Melodies across the trees.

The sun, a conductor in the sky,
Leads the earth, as birds learn to fly.
Each note a story, sweet and true,
An orchestra of morning dew.

Flowers open, bright and fair,
Filling the air with fragrant care.
Each petal strums a gentle chord,
In the symphony, we're adored.

Streams hum softly as they wend,
A soothing tune, the heart's own friend.
Nature's symphony, rich and bold,
In every silence, stories told.

With each new dawn, our spirits rise,
Embracing life beneath the skies.
In this symphony, we belong,
Crafting dreams with every song.

The Awakening of Starlit Fantasies

Beneath the canvas of night skies,
Dreams awaken in silent sighs.
Whispers dance like gentle breeze,
Carrying hopes through swaying trees.

Stars begin their timeless song,
In the darkness, where we belong.
A symphony of cosmic light,
Guiding our hearts through the night.

Visions swirl in silver streams,
Painting portraits of lost dreams.
The moon smiles, a watchful eye,
As secrets drift and softly fly.

With every twinkle, stories bloom,
Sparking joy, dispelling gloom.
The universe wraps us tight,
In the embrace of twinkling light.

Awakening as dawn creeps near,
Starlit fantasies disappear.
Yet in the heart, they remain,
A gentle echo, a sweet refrain.

In the Embrace of Daylight's Kiss

Morning breaks with tender grace,
Sunbeams dance on nature's face.
A golden warmth begins to rise,
Painting colors in the skies.

Birds sing sweetly to the morn,
With every note, a day reborn.
The world awakens, fresh and bright,
In the sacred glow of light.

Mountains bathe in daylight's glow,
Fields of green in vibrant flow.
Every leaf, a diamond spun,
In the embrace of the new sun.

Moments linger, soft and pure,
Daylight's love, a gentle cure.
Each breath filled with promise clear,
In the warmth, we shed our fear.

As shadows fade and spirits rise,
We find our truth beneath vast skies.
In this dance of light and bliss,
We cherish every day's sweet kiss.

Footprints on the Canvas of Life

Each step we take, a mark we leave,
In a world that seeks to believe.
Footprints tell the tales we weave,
A journey etched, our hearts retrieve.

Paths entwined through joy and strife,
Each moment shapes the canvas life.
Brushstrokes of laughter, tears, and pain,
Color the memories that remain.

With every stumble, we learn to stand,
We write our stories with trembling hand.
The canvas stretches, vast and wide,
A testament to our life's ride.

In shades of love, hope, and grace,
We find our place in time and space.
Every footprint, a story told,
A legacy of hearts bold.

As we gaze back on roads we've roamed,
In every step, we find our home.
Life's canvas painted with care,
In every footprint, love we share.

Serenading the Rising Sun

As dawn unfolds with gentle breath,
Nature stirs, defying death.
Birds awaken, singing tunes,
Celebrating light from glowing moons.

The horizon blushes, warm and bright,
Awakening realms with golden light.
Every shadow begins to flee,
In jubilant dance, the world feels free.

Morning whispers through the trees,
A serenade carried by the breeze.
Flowers bloom in radiant hues,
Grateful for the day's debut.

With every ray, hopes ignite,
Promises swirl in pure delight.
As the sun ascends up high,
Dreams take flight into the sky.

The day unfolds, a tale anew,
A symphony of hope in view.
In the embrace of morning's grace,
We find our dreams in this warm place.

Whispers of a New Beginning

In the dawn's soft light,
Dreams start to take flight.
Silent hopes unfold,
A tale yet untold.

The air is filled with grace,
Time begins to embrace.
Each step feels so bright,
Guided by inner light.

Leaves flutter in cheer,
The path now feels clear.
With courage, we rise,
To touch the vast skies.

New colors paint the day,
As doubts fade away.
With trust in our hearts,
The journey departs.

Together we find peace,
As worries all cease.
The whispers ignite,
A new dawn in sight.

Joyful Journeys Beyond the Cloud

Beneath a sky so wide,
We wander side by side.
Each moment, a treasure,
Wrapped in pure pleasure.

The sun's warm embrace,
Brings smiles to each face.
With laughter, we soar,
To lands unexplored.

Through valleys and streams,
We dance in our dreams.
With every heartbeat,
Adventure's our seat.

Clouds part with a smile,
We travel each mile.
With spirits so free,
We laugh by the sea.

Through horizons aglow,
Our hearts feel the flow.
In joy, we unite,
Chasing pure delight.

Beyond the Veil of Night

When shadows softly creep,
And the world falls asleep.
Stars whisper their tales,
Through moonlit veils and gales.

In silence, secrets breathe,
As dreams begin to weave.
The heart starts to roam,
In realms far from home.

Mysteries awake,
With every small quake.
In darkness, we find,
A light in the mind.

Through twilight's embrace,
We search for a space.
Where hope shines anew,
In shades of deep blue.

When dawn breaks the spell,
With stories to tell.
Beyond night we rise,
To greet the day's skies.

When Hope Takes Flight

With wings that unfurl,
Amidst a vast swirl.
We grasp at the sky,
As dreams pass us by.

A whisper of dawn,
Encouragement drawn.
With each step we take,
The world feels awake.

Through storms and through strife,
We dance with our life.
Hope's beacon shines bright,
Guiding us through the night.

When worries dissolve,
And courage evolves.
Together we chase,
A bright, open space.

In the warmth of the sun,
New journeys begun.
When hope takes its flight,
All darkness turns light.

A Tapestry Woven with Joyful Whispers

Threads of laughter in the air,
Colors dancing everywhere,
Hearts entwined in soft embrace,
Joyful whispers find their place.

Beneath the stars, stories shared,
Moments cherished, souls laid bare,
In the glow of twilight's hue,
Friendships blossom, deep and true.

Woven dreams in vibrant strands,
Crafted softly by tender hands,
Each knot a promise, brightly spun,
A tapestry of love begun.

In every fold, a secret kept,
Of all the tears and laughter wept,
Echoes linger, fond and dear,
In this fabric, joy draws near.

A quilt of moments, stitched with care,
A timeless gift we all can share,
Forever wrapped in memories bright,
A tapestry woven with pure delight.

Serene Valleys of Blissful Anticipation

In valleys deep, where silence reigns,
Nature whispers soft refrains,
Colors bloom in gentle light,
A canvas painted, pure and bright.

With every step, the heart takes flight,
Towards horizons kissed by light,
Dreams unfurl like petals fair,
In these valleys, hope fills the air.

Mountains cradle skies of blue,
With clouds that drift, they reshape too,
A landscape rich with mysteries,
Inviting souls to wander free.

Beneath the trees, a calm embrace,
Where time slows down, and fears erase,
In sacred spaces, peace we find,
A promise made, to love unbind.

So let us stroll through gentle grace,
In valleys serene, our hearts shall race,
Blissful anticipation swells,
A symphony where nature dwells.

The Journey Towards Luminescent Futures

With every step, we forge our way,
Through shadows cast by doubt's array,
The road unfolds beneath our dreams,
Illuminated by hopeful beams.

Together we chase the rising sun,
Awakening hearts, our journey's begun,
With every challenge, lessons grow,
Guiding stars in twilight's glow.

Paths may twist, and may divide,
Yet in our souls, we shall confide,
For within each turn lies strength anew,
A destiny crafted, bright and true.

Embrace the winds, let courage soar,
In the unknown, we'll find much more,
With visions clear, we shall ignite,
A future bathed in golden light.

So onward we march, no fears to hide,
Together in love, as our faithful guide,
The journey unfolds, the world awaits,
Towards luminescent, open gates.

Dreams Stirring in the Wake of Dawn

As night departs, the light unfolds,
In morning's grace, a tale retold,
Dreams awaken, fluttering near,
Whispers soft, for all to hear.

Golden rays through windows seep,
Calling forth the hearts from sleep,
Each promise glimmers, bright and warm,
In this moment, new hopes form.

A canvas fresh, the day begins,
With every heartbeat, life within,
Take a breath, embrace the light,
Let your spirit take to flight.

In the stillness, magic brews,
As dawn's embrace invites our dues,
For every dream that stirs in light,
Holds the promise of delight.

So rise with hope, embrace the day,
Let dreams abound, come what may,
In the wake of dawn's sweet song,
Together we shall journey strong.

Soaring Spirits in the Realm of Imagination

In the sky of dreams we fly,
Wings of wonder, never shy.
Clouds of color, vivid and bright,
Chasing whispers of delight.

Thoughts like rivers, flowing free,
Crafting worlds for you and me.
Stars are stories yet untold,
In this realm, our hearts behold.

From the depths of our desire,
Burns the flame of purest fire.
We create as we believe,
In the magic we conceive.

Journey forth on winds so sweet,
Every heartbeat, a new beat.
In imagination's embrace,
We find our spirit's rightful place.

Soaring high on dreams unbound,
In this space, we are profound.
Let the visions take their flight,
In the canvas of the night.

The Canvas of Exuberant Journeys

Upon the canvas, colors blend,
Every stroke, a tale to send.
With each hue, adventures start,
Paint the journey from the heart.

Every shade, a step we've known,
Mapping paths to seeds we've sown.
In the midst of vibrant schemes,
We dance along the threads of dreams.

Brushes dipped in joy and cheer,
Every moment, crystal clear.
As we wander, laugh and play,
Life unfolds in bright array.

Beyond each twist, a story waits,
Open doors and endless gates.
Every journey, bold and bright,
Guided by the endless light.

Together we paint the sky,
With our hopes, we'll learn to fly.
In this canvas, tales we weave,
A masterpiece we all believe.

Boundless Views of a Heart's Desire

With each sunrise, dreams arise,
A tapestry before our eyes.
Waves of longing crash ashore,
Whispers beckon to explore.

Mountains rise, the valleys call,
In this quest, we seek it all.
Vistas stretch, horizons wide,
In this journey, we confide.

Every turn reveals a view,
Moments cherished, tried and true.
Heartbeats sing with sweet release,
Finding in the journey, peace.

As we chase what sets us free,
Boundless paths, our destiny.
In the echoes of our quest,
We find our truth, our very best.

Heart aflame, the world expands,
Together we will make our plans.
In the quest for what's admired,
We embrace our heart's desire.

Reveling in the Glow of Aspiration

In the dawn of dreams we rise,
Chasing sparks that fill the skies.
Every heartbeat, a step we take,
In the light, we boldly wake.

Radiant stars of hope ignite,
Guiding us through the dark night.
With our wishes, we ignite,
In the glow, we find our light.

Each pursuit, a flame within,
Burning bright, where dreams begin.
In the dance of joy and grace,
We discover our own space.

Feel the warmth of passion's glow,
As we strive, our spirits grow.
In the moments, joy we trace,
Boldly moving, we embrace.

So let us soar on wings of fire,
With each dream, we dare aspire.
In the tapestry we weave,
Together, we shall truly believe.

Magic in the Light of Day

In the morning, golden rays,
Whispers of hope, a brand new phase.
Birds sing sweetly, skies so blue,
Nature's canvas, fresh and true.

Soft shadows play on the ground,
Every moment, beauty found.
Laughter dances in the breeze,
Life awakens with such ease.

Time drips slowly, joy ignites,
Chasing dreams with pure delights.
Every heart beats in a flow,
Under sun's warm, gentle glow.

Clouds drift by like cotton candy,
Moments cherished, sweet and dandy.
A world alive, vibrant and grand,
In the light, we take our stand.

Together under skies so wide,
Finding magic in every stride.
With each sunrise, love and play,
Unfolding dreams in light of day.

Dreams That Dance on Gentle Breezes

Whispers echo through the night,
Carried softly, pure delight.
Winds of hope, they sway and turn,
In their arms, our dreams will burn.

Silver stars like diamonds shine,
Guiding paths through stories divine.
In a dance, the shadows twirl,
Magic swirls in every whirl.

Floating wishes on moonlit streams,
Awake, we are in vivid dreams.
Hearts united, spirits free,
Life unfolds in harmony.

Gentle breezes kiss our souls,
Lifting spirits towards our goals.
With every sigh, we take a chance,
As our hopes begin to dance.

In twilight's glow, we find our way,
Lost in dreams both night and day.
Forever chasing what feels right,
As dreams that dance, ignite the night.

Colors of a Vibrant Tomorrow

Radiant hues paint the sky,
With every dawn, we learn to fly.
Brushstrokes bold, love intertwined,
In every heart, dreams shall bind.

Fields of flowers stretch so wide,
Beneath the sun, our hopes abide.
Petals flutter, colors blend,
Nature's art, a perfect trend.

Golden sunsets, crimson flames,
Every moment, sparks new games.
In this world where colors thrive,
Hope and joy will always drive.

With our hearts full of desire,
We ignite the world with fire.
Painting visions, bright and clear,
In tomorrow, we'll persevere.

As shadows fade and dreams take flight,
We embrace a future bright.
Colors shine in all we do,
Crafting life in vibrant hue.

Notes of Bliss in the Morning Air

Morning rises, soft and low,
Echoes of joy in each soft glow.
Birdsong weaves a gentle tune,
Awakening dreams beneath the moon.

Sipping coffee, warm and sweet,
Enjoying life in every beat.
With each note, hope is renewed,
In the air, a sweet mood.

Sunlight dances on the dew,
Every moment feels like new.
Whispers of love fill the air,
Notes of bliss everywhere.

Clouds drift slowly, a tender sigh,
Painting stories in the sky.
Each new day, a song we share,
In the morning, love is rare.

Melodies of laughter blend,
In this moment, hearts ascend.
Let the music always stay,
In the notes of bliss, we play.

The Symphony of Tomorrow

In the quiet of the night,
Dreams take flight, casting light.
Voices blend in harmony,
A tune of hope, wild and free.

Stars above begin to glow,
Guiding paths where we might go.
Fingers dance on velvet keys,
Creating songs that soothe the seas.

As the morning breaks anew,
All our fears we must undo.
Notes of courage swell and rise,
Unleashing joy, reaching skies.

Every heart, a vibrant sound,
Melodies that will astound.
Together we'll weave our fate,
In this symphony, elevate.

Moments shared, a sweet embrace,
In this dreamscape, find our place.
Waves of music, pure delight,
A future bright, vast as night.

Boundless Skies of Delight

Underneath the endless blue,
Dreams come true as spirits flew.
Winds of change whisper and sway,
Carving paths where hearts can play.

Fields of golden sun embrace,
Every shadow finds its place.
With laughter ringing through the air,
Joy unfolds, beyond compare.

Clouds like cotton drift above,
Carrying wishes, peace, and love.
Each horizon opens wide,
Welcoming hope on every ride.

When the twilight paints the scene,
Stars awaken, soft and keen.
In this expanse, we unite,
Boundless skies of pure delight.

Together, hand in hand we soar,
Through the vastness, we explore.
Dreamers' hearts shall never tire,
In these skies, we rise, aspire.

Echoes of Laughter on the Wind

Softly whispers through the trees,
Laughter dances with the breeze.
Every note, a memory,
Tracing back to you and me.

In the vale, where shadows play,
Echoes bright the skies today.
Each delight a fleeting song,
Binding hearts, where we belong.

Through the fields, our voices blend,
Nature's chorus never ends.
Every giggle, every cheer,
Paints the world when you are near.

As the sun begins to set,
Moments cherished, none regret.
In the twilight, joy we send,
Echoes of laughter on the wind.

Time may pass, but love remains,
Carried forth through joyful strains.
In our hearts, the songs will live,
In these echoes, we forgive.

Radiant Visions of Dawn

When the morning lights the way,
Hope awakens with the day.
Colors burst in splendor bright,
Chasing shadows, bringing light.

Every petal softly wakes,
Songs of nature, sweetly breaks.
In the glow, our dreams align,
Radiant visions, pure and fine.

Golden rays touch every stream,
Waking life within the dream.
As the world begins to sing,
We find joy in everything.

Hearts ignite with each new morn,
From the night, new paths are born.
In the stillness, find the sound,
Of radiant visions all around.

Together, let our spirits soar,
In this light, forever more.
New beginnings, fresh and grand,
Guided by each loving hand.

Kaleidoscope of Wishes

In the garden of dreams we gather,
Colors twist and turn like whispers.
Each wish a petal, bright and tender,
Spinning tales of light forever.

Underneath a sky so vast,
We cast our hopes like autumn leaves.
Time flows slow, moments fade fast,
In this realm, our heart believes.

Fragments of laughter fill the air,
Twirling memories come alive.
With every thought and heartfelt prayer,
In this dance, our spirits thrive.

Let the world see through our eyes,
The beauty found in shades of grace.
Every dream a star that flies,
In unity, we find our place.

Together we weave the threads of light,
A tapestry of dreams awaits.
In this kaleidoscope, so bright,
A symphony of hopeful fates.

The Light that Calls Us Home

When shadows stretch across the land,
A beacon glows with gentle grace.
It reaches out, a guiding hand,
In every heart, it finds its place.

We wander far on winding roads,
Yet hear the whispers, soft and clear.
The light that leads where love explodes,
A warm embrace, forever near.

In twilight's hush, it starts to sing,
Notes of solace fill the air.
The night unfolds, its tapestry,
And hope is woven with such care.

Across the fields of dreams untold,
We find our way, step by step.
The light within begins to unfold,
A promise made, our hearts adept.

Return to love, the path is bright,
With every star, our spirits roam.
Together in this endless night,
The light that calls us, leads us home.

Dreamscapes of a Brighter Day

In the whispers of dawn's embrace,
Dreams awaken with a gentle sigh.
The world unfurls, a vibrant place,
  With open hearts, we dare to fly.

Colors dance on the morning dew,
  Painting visions in the sky.
Each moment holds a chance anew,
To catch our dreams as they float by.

With every step, we forge a path,
Among the clouds where hopes arise.
In laughter's echo, feel the warmth,
  As day begins to light our skies.

The shadows fade, giving way to light,
  In this dance, our spirits sway.
Embrace the dawn, the future bright,
  In dreamscapes, we find our way.

Let us wander through fields of gold,
  Hand in hand, united we stay.
In the tapestry of life foretold,
  Together we build a brighter day.

Embracing the Morning Glow

Awake to the warmth of sunlit beams,
Each ray a promise, soft and sweet.
In the hush of dawn, the world redeems,
With open arms, our hearts repeat.

The sky ignites with hues of grace,
A canvas brushed with tender light.
With every breath, we find our place,
In the magic of this morning bright.

Birds serenade the waking hour,
Their songs a melody divine.
In the bloom of each vibrant flower,
Nature's beauty, pure and fine.

Together, we rise with spirits high,
In this moment, we belong.
With every heartbeat, hear the sigh,
Of dreams that stretch and grow strong.

Embrace the day, let worries fade,
In this glow, our fears let go.
With love, the dawn's sweet serenade,
We dance in joy, embracing the glow.

Where Stars and Dreams Converge

In the night sky, wishes fly,
Whispers of dreams, they softly sigh.
Stars twinkle bright, a cosmic dance,
Guiding our hearts toward a chance.

Galaxies swirl in a velvet sea,
Infinite paths await you and me.
Where hopes align under moonlit beams,
Magic unfolds in our wildest dreams.

The constellations weave our fate,
Each shining light, a story innate.
In the silence, hear the heart's call,
Together we rise, we will not fall.

As dawn approaches, shadows wane,
Eclipsed by love, dispelling pain.
Together we journey, hand in hand,
Where stars and dreams forever stand.

In this sacred space, we belong,
A harmony found in a celestial song.
Always within, our spirits merge,
In the universe vast, where dreams converge.

Heartbeats in the Dawn

As the sun rises, a new day breaks,
Whispers of light in the stillness wakes.
The world stretches out, alive and bright,
Heartbeats echo through the morning light.

Golden rays touch the dewy grass,
Embracing the moments as they pass.
Each breath a promise, fresh and clear,
In the dawn's embrace, we shed our fear.

Birds take flight with a joyful song,
Nature awakens, where we belong.
With every heartbeat, excitement swells,
In the magic of dawn, our spirit tells.

Together we stand, facing the sky,
With hopes that soar, like birds on high.
In this fragile moment, love unfolds,
As heartbeats whisper tales untold.

In the stillness, we find our grace,
Each dawn a reminder, a warm embrace.
With open hearts, we chase the light,
In the rhythm of life, every heartbeat bright.

Elements of Joy in the Sunlight

Beneath the sky, where laughter shines,
Joy blooms brightly in vivid lines.
Sun-kissed moments, pure delight,
Unexpected wonders ignite the night.

The gentle breeze whispers secrets sweet,
Nature's dance, a rhythmic beat.
Dancing daisies, a bright bouquet,
In the sunlight's glow, worries decay.

Colors erupt in a vibrant swirl,
Each petal unfurls, a bright new world.
Laughter rings out, like chimes in tune,
Celebrating life beneath the moon.

Time slows down in this golden haze,
Every heartbeat a precious phrase.
In the warmth of the sun, we feel alive,
In the elements of joy, we thrive.

Together we bask in the warmth's embrace,
Finding bliss in this sacred space.
With every smile, we light the way,
In the sunlight's glow, we choose to stay.

Link to the Light

In shadows deep, a flicker glows,
A gentle guide that softly shows.
The passage clear, through night we tread,
Finding courage where fears are shed.

Tangled branches, yet we press on,
With every step, our hearts are drawn.
A whisper calls from the beyond,
Leading us forth to dreams that bond.

Through trials faced, we'll stand upright,
With love as our beacon, a powerful light.
In unity's strength, we rise above,
Holding tight to hope and love.

With every heartbeat, a promise made,
In the dark, we will not fade.
Together we'll forge this pathway bright,
As souls entwined, we link to the light.

As dawn breaks forth, shadows retreat,
In luminous glow, our joy is complete.
A bond unbroken, forever to stay,
In the embrace of light, we find our way.

The Canvas of Daydreams

On the canvas of thought, colors blend,
Brush strokes of wishes that time can't mend.
Whispers of silence create vivid scenes,
In corners of joy, where no one intervenes.

Each shade tells a story, a hope to be found,
In realms of imagination, where dreams know no bound.
The palette of moments, both tender and bright,
Draws us away from the pull of the night.

As shadows retreat, and daylight unveils,
The art of tomorrow in soft, swirling trails.
With every new dawn, a masterpiece starts,
The canvas of daydreams, a dance of our hearts.

Morning's Promise in Bloom

Dew-kissed petals stretch and yawn,
Welcoming light, heralding dawn.
A symphony whispers in soft, warm hues,
Nature's embrace, a vibrant muse.

With each gentle breeze, the blossoms sway,
Morning's promise, a bright display.
Colors awaken, brightening the scene,
All life rejoices, refreshed and serene.

Birdsong dances through the crisp air,
Beckoning hearts to awaken, to care.
In gardens of hope, life writes its tune,
Unfurling dreams like flowers in bloom.

Echoes of Tomorrow's Laughter

In the echoes of laughter, futures collide,
Whispers of joy on the shimmering tide.
Memories linger, bright glimmers of cheer,
As days weave together, year after year.

Bubbles of glee rise into the air,
Carrying dreams, sweet moments to share.
The clock ticks softly, but still we find ways,
To cherish the now in the light of our days.

With each joyful glance, futures align,
Building tomorrow on moments divine.
In laughter's embrace, we find our sweet song,
Echoing brightly, where our hearts belong.

Celestial Whispers of Contentment

Underneath the vast, twinkling sky,
Celestial whispers, faint and shy.
Stars hum a tune of serene delight,
Guiding our souls through the velvet night.

Each twinkle a promise, a soft serenade,
In the warmth of the cosmos, our worries fade.
Dreams drift like clouds, so gentle, so free,
Painting the heavens with hopes yet to be.

In silence, we gather the glow from above,
Wrapped in the essence of peace and love.
Celestial whispers, a soothing embrace,
Infusing our beings with infinite grace.

Symphony of Radiant Rebirth

In the hush of dawn, the world awakes,
Soft light spills gold on shimmering lakes.
Whispers of hope dance through the air,
Each note a promise, beyond despair.

Blossoms unfurl with a vibrant sigh,
Painting the sky as the larks fly high.
Nature's canvas, stroked with delight,
A symphony born from the quiet night.

A heartbeat echoes in the blossomed trees,
Tales of renewal carried by the breeze.
Every petal shines with a secret glow,
In harmony with life's endless flow.

Through valleys deep, the river flows clear,
Reflecting laughter, washing away fear.
In every ripple, a story unfolds,
Of resilience woven in threads of gold.

Each moment cherished, a treasure to keep,
As dreams awaken from their slumbering sleep.
Together they dance in the morning's embrace,
A radiant rebirth, a timeless grace.

The Resilience of Daylight's Dreams

When shadows linger and twilight creeps,
The heart holds tight to the promise it keeps.
In the stillness, hope begins to gleam,
Awakening softly from a distant dream.

Sunrise unfolds like the petals of spring,
Each golden ray an enchanting fling.
The world bathed bright in a luminous hue,
As daylight weaves its magic anew.

Even the storms that may tear at the sky,
Can't dim the light, nor dampen the high.
For in every challenge that life may bestow,
Resilience fuels the fire to grow.

A symphony played on the strings of the heart,
Reviving the dreams that set us apart.
Each heartbeat a note in the song we compose,
In the radiant glow where our spirit flows.

As daylight dances on the edges of night,
We'll follow our dreams, embracing the light.
With courage ignited and purpose in sight,
We soar through the heavens, hearts taking flight.

A Flourish of Joy on New Adventures

In the dawn's embrace, a new path unfolds,
A tapestry rich with stories untold.
Every turn beckons with laughter and cheer,
As we step boldly into the year.

With each new horizon, a thrill in our veins,
We chase the sun through the wild golden plains.
The sky whispers secrets on the winds that blow,
Guiding our feet where the wildflowers grow.

Adventures await, painting joy in our souls,
In the art of living, we glimmer and roll.
Collecting the moments like jewels in a chest,
Finding our peace in each joyful quest.

The laughter that echoes, the friend's gentle hand,
In the weave of our journey, together we stand.
With courage and wonder lighting our way,
We hold tightly to dreams that invite us to play.

In this dance of life, let our spirits be free,
As we step through the world, just you and me.
With every adventure, a flourish takes flight,
Bringing joy to our hearts, like stars in the night.

A Canvas of Infinite Possibilities

In hues of blue and shades of gold,
The dreams of our hearts begin to unfold.
With every stroke, a story we weave,
In the art of creation, we truly believe.

Colors clash and harmony sings,
In the vision of art, the soul takes wings.
Each brush, a portal to realms unknown,
A canvas of life where seeds are sown.

Whispers of fate in strokes divine,
We dance with the brush on this palette of time.
Every splash is a chance to explore,
Infinite dreams waiting at the door.

In the silence of thought, ideas ignite,
Painted with passion, bold and bright.
The world is a canvas, vast and grand,
A masterpiece waiting for our hand.

As colors blend and new shades appear,
We find our purpose, we conquer fear.
Life's an art, a beautiful creed,
In its vibrant strokes, our hearts are freed.

Sunlit Paths of Happiness

Beneath the azure sky so wide,
We wander together, side by side.
With laughter ringing in the breeze,
Sunlit paths lead to moments that please.

Golden rays dance on the ground,
In every step, joy can be found.
With every sunset, a promise we make,
To cherish the journeys, the memories we take.

Fields of daisies sway in tune,
Under the glow of the gentle moon.
In each blossom, our hopes intertwine,
In the garden of life, love's light will shine.

The warmth of friendship, a guiding star,
No matter how near, no matter how far.
Together we rise; together we fall,
On sunlit paths, we'll always stand tall.

With hearts wide open, we embrace each day,
In the sun's embrace, we'll find our way.
Life's a treasure, let's sing it out loud,
On sunlit paths, forever we're proud.

Unfolding the Wings of Imagination

In the quiet corners of our mind,
Endless wonders are waiting to find.
With every thought, a flicker of light,
Unfolding our wings, we take flight.

Clouds of dreams drift softly away,
In the canvas of night, we dance and play.
With whispers of magic in the air,
Imagination blooms, vivid and rare.

Beyond the horizon, where hopes reside,
We soar on the wings of what's deep inside.
Each fantasy blooms like petals unfurled,
In the garden of dreams, we create our world.

With courage ignited, we chase the stars,
Breaking the silence, we conquer our scars.
Through pathways of wonder, we journey on,
Unfolding the wings till the break of dawn.

In the tapestry woven with threads of delight,
Each vision, a chance to glimpse the light.
Let's embrace the magic, the boundless scene,
Unfolding the wings of imagination's dream.

The Garden of Endless Dreams

In the garden of hopes, the flowers bloom,
Each petal holds stories that chase the gloom.
Under the sun, our wishes take flight,
In the heart of the garden, dreams feel right.

With every season, new colors arise,
Sown from the seeds of the wisest of ties.
In the fragrance of joy, we find our way,
The garden whispers, come out and play.

Butterflies flutter, a dance in the air,
As laughter and love fill the spaces we share.
In each vibrant bloom, a tale is spun,
In this enchanted place, we become one.

Amidst rustling leaves, our spirits soar,
Embracing the magic of what's in store.
With every heartbeat, we nurture the dream,
In the garden's embrace, life's a gleam.

So let us wander, hand in hand,
In the garden of love, where dreams expand.
With every whisper of the gentle breeze,
The garden of endless dreams brings us peace.

A Journey into the Sunrise

As dawn breaks softly on the sea,
The world awakens, wild and free.
Colors spill like dreams untold,
Whispers of warmth in hues of gold.

Footsteps follow the sandy shore,
Each wave echoes tales of yore.
The sun climbs high with gentle grace,
Guiding hearts to a brighter space.

Birds take flight on wings of hope,
In the morning light, we learn to cope.
With every ray that paints the sky,
We find the strength to soar and fly.

Moments pass like grains of sand,
We reach for dreams with open hands.
Together, we chase the rising light,
Embracing the magic of the night.

Onward we travel, hand in hand,
Through the whispers of this land.
The journey paints our souls anew,
In every shade of every view.

Wings of Light and Laughter

Beneath the sky of golden beams,
We dance and play, lost in dreams.
Laughter echoes through the air,
With joy that glows and hearts laid bare.

The sunlit glades, where shadows play,
Invite us forth to laugh and stay.
In every chuckle, magic flows,
The world awakens, love only grows.

Wings of light begin to spread,
Carrying wishes where we tread.
We float on breezes, soft and warm,
Our spirits lifted, free from harm.

In this embrace, we share our dreams,
A tapestry of golden beams.
Together we rise, unafraid to glide,
With laughter strong, we'll turn the tide.

Through every challenge, hand in hand,
We find a way, we boldly stand.
United in spirit, hearts afire,
In wings of light, we soar higher.

Seeds of Joy in the Dawn

To wake with hope at break of day,
Is to cast worries far away.
In every seed that finds the ground,
A spark of joy is waiting, found.

The morning dew, a gentle kiss,
Nurtures dreams, a quiet bliss.
With each petal that starts to bloom,
We feel the rise of joy consume.

The sun will shine, the sky will clear,
A promise whispered, loud and near.
With each new breath, we plant the seed,
In gardens deep, where souls are freed.

Nature dances to a joyful tune,
Under the watchful eye of the moon.
In every heartbeat, hope will soar,
As seeds of joy break through the floor.

We gather strength from what we've sown,
In golden fields, we've brightly grown.
Together we feel the dawn's embrace,
In every smile, a warm, safe place.

The Dance of Dreams and Reality

In twilight's glow, our dreams take flight,
Painting visions in soft twilight.
The lines blur where we dare to tread,
In the magic woven by dreams we've fed.

We twirl 'neath stars, our hearts entwined,
A dance of fate, beautifully designed.
In every step, the world we create,
Together we weave our destined fate.

In the pulse of night, we reach for more,
With every whisper, we open the door.
Between the dreams and what is real,
We find the essence of how to feel.

Time melts away in this sacred space,
In the waltz of wonder, we find our place.
As shadows flicker, the night unfolds,
A tapestry of stories waiting to be told.

Through the dance of dreams, we see anew,
The colors of life in every hue.
To dream and to live, hand in hand we roam,
In this dance of life, we find our home.

The Melody of Morning Dreams

Whispers of dawn begin to rise,
Softly painting the waking skies.
Singing birds in gentle flight,
Crafting tunes of pure delight.

Golden rays through leaves will creep,
Awakening the world from sleep.
Each note played, a sweet refrain,
A serenade to ease the pain.

Dew-kissed petals, fresh and bright,
Reflecting joy in morning light.
Nature's symphony unfolds,
In quiet moments, peace beholds.

Breezes dance through fields of green,
Carrying dreams yet to be seen.
Echoes of hopes softly blend,
In the melody, hearts ascend.

As shadows fade and daylight wakes,
Every heartbeat gently shakes.
In this dawn, dreams come alive,
In morning's arms, we thrive and strive.

Splashing Colors on Life's Canvas

With each stroke, the world ignites,
A tapestry of vibrant sights.
Rainbows spill from brush to ground,
In chaos, beauty can be found.

Crimson hues of passion's fire,
Brush away the shades of mire.
Sapphire blues of calm embrace,
Bring serenity to this space.

Golden yellows, warmth they bring,
Harvest joy in colors' swing.
Emerald greens that softly sway,
Reflect the life of each new day.

In the painting, stories tell,
Of loves, of dreams, and wishes fell.
Splashing colors, bold and free,
Illuminate the soul's decree.

As the canvas comes alive,
In each hue, our spirits thrive.
Every color, every line,
Creates a world that's truly divine.

Embracing the Day's Embrace

Morning light breaks on my skin,
A soft touch where dreams begin.
The world awakes, a gentle sigh,
Under the vast and gleaming sky.

Coffee brews, the aroma flows,
Carrying hope as the day grows.
Every moment, a chance to start,
With open arms and an eager heart.

Sunlit paths where shadows play,
Invite the new, embrace the day.
Every heartbeat, every breath,
A reminder of life's depth.

Nature whispers, sweet and clear,
Inviting us to draw near.
In every leaf, in every sound,
The magic of life can be found.

At day's end, the stars will rise,
A blanket of dreams in evening skies.
Embracing moments, holding tight,
We dance with joy into the night.

The Horizon of Heartfelt Wishes

Beyond the hills where dreams take flight,
Lies a horizon glowing bright.
Wishes whispered on the breeze,
Carried far with graceful ease.

Each star above, a hope in sight,
Guides us through the velvet night.
With every wish, a chance to grow,
In the depths of our hearts, they glow.

Waves of longing crash and swell,
Like secrets only time can tell.
Past the bounds where shadows hide,
Wishes linger, dreams abide.

In twilight's hush, the sky will weep,
As heartfelt wishes softly seep.
Into the fabric of our fate,
Crafting stories, small and great.

So gaze beyond the setting sun,
For every wish, the journey's begun.
On the horizon, dreams will bloom,
Casting light in the darkest room.

Upon the Crest of Optimism

Upon the crest, we rise so high,
With dreams that dance beneath the sky.
Hope whispers soft, a gentle breeze,
Guiding our hearts with joyful ease.

Each step we take, a leap of faith,
Embracing life, a sweet embrace.
The sun will shine upon our face,
As we find strength in every place.

With every dawn, new light will break,
Awakening hope with each heartache.
Together we stand, hand in hand,
Creating joy across the land.

In laughter's song, we find our way,
The promise of a brighter day.
Through storms we'll dance, through shadows play,
On optimism, we shall stay.

So rise with me, let's touch the skies,
For in our hearts, the spirit flies.
In every breath, a chance to dream,
Life's sweetest moments, ever gleam.

Recipes of Joy for the Soul

A sprinkle of laughter, a dash of cheer,
Mix in some love, hold it near.
Stir with kindness, let it blend,
Serve it warm to every friend.

Add in some dreams, big and bold,
A cup of memories, stories told.
Pour in the courage, let it rise,
Taste the magic, feel the skies.

Set the table with gratitude's grace,
Invite the weary to a warm embrace.
Season with hope, a pinch of peace,
Let all worries and sorrows cease.

Bake under the warmth of the sun,
Gather together, let joy be spun.
Savor the moments, one and all,
For recipes of joy will never fall.

So share your dish, let laughter flow,
In every heart, let kindness grow.
With every taste, a tale we weave,
A feast of love, we shall believe.

Pillars of Light and Hope

In the midst of night, they stand so tall,
Pillars of light, guiding us all.
With every flame, a story told,
Of strength and courage, brave and bold.

They light the path we choose to tread,
Whispers of dreams, softly spread.
Through every trial, through tears we cope,
Pillars of faith, the roots of hope.

Under their watch, worries fade,
With every promise, fears are laid.
In shadows deep, we find our way,
As light endures, night turns to day.

Together we rise, hands intertwined,
With hearts aglow, our spirits aligned.
For in this journey, we will discover,
Pillars of light; we are all each other.

So trust in the light that shines so bright,
In every heart, ignite the fight.
Through storms we walk, with hope in sight,
Together forever, arms held tight.

The Awakening of Bright Horizons

With dawn's first light, the world awakes,
Colors dance as the morning breaks.
Horizons stretch with promise anew,
Whispers of dreams in skies so blue.

Each day unfolds, a canvas wide,
Adventures await, no need to hide.
In every heartbeat, the pulse of life,
Through joys and sorrows, peace or strife.

The mountains call, the rivers sing,
Nature's chorus, celebrating spring.
With open hearts, we welcome change,
In the vast expanse, so beautiful, strange.

Together we'll chase the sun's bright rays,
In laughter's echoes, we'll find our ways.
To every horizon, our spirits fly,
In the arms of hope, we learn to try.

So let us gather, hand in hand,
Embracing life, a promise planned.
In every dawn, a chance to thrive,
Awakening bright horizons, alive.

A Journey Through Joyful Whispers

In the quiet of the dawn,
Soft whispers float on air,
Each note is filled with gold,
A promise lives within the prayer.

The path ahead is bright,
With laughter in the breeze,
Every step a dance,
Like leaves upon the trees.

Eyes sparkle with delight,
As dreams take gentle flight,
Hearts beating in sync,
In the morning light.

Moments weave like thread,
In colors bold and new,
Together we shall tread,
In joy, deep and true.

With each echoing cheer,
Our spirits intertwine,
In this realm of love,
Eternal, so divine.

Celestial Euphoria Unfolding

Stars twinkle in the night,
A cosmic dance above,
Each sparkle tells a tale,
Whispers of endless love.

Galaxies align with grace,
In rhythm, hearts do sway,
The universe expands,
Guiding us on our way.

Moonlight bathes the ground,
In silver hues so bright,
Our souls begin to soar,
Eclipsing all the night.

Songs of joy resound,
In echoes deeply felt,
Each chord a gentle hug,
In harmony, we melt.

With each breath of joy,
We reach for skies so wide,
Euphoria unfolds,
Our spirits set to glide.

Tides of Elation at Day's Break

The sun peeks o'er the sea,
Painting waves with gold,
In the warmth of its embrace,
Joyful stories unfold.

Every crest and every fall,
A heartbeat of the shore,
Hope sails on each current,
Yearning for something more.

Seagulls dance above,
Their cries a sweet refrain,
As the world awakens,
To the promise of no pain.

Footprints in the sand,
Mark the moments dear,
With each tide that washes,
We shed all of our fear.

In this dawn's embrace,
We find our spirits free,
For the tides of elation,
Flow through you and me.

The Rhythm of Hopeful Hearts

In the silence of the night,
A heartbeat starts to rise,
Each pulse a quiet dream,
Underneath the starlit skies.

Rhythms dance in shadows,
Melodies softly played,
Every hope resounds,
In the choices that we've made.

With each breath, we march on,
In sync with life's embrace,
Carving paths of love,
In the universe's space.

Hands joined in unity,
Building bridges of light,
Together, we create,
A future shining bright.

In the tapestry of time,
Our hearts beat as one,
In the rhythm of life's song,
Hope is never done.

Letting Laughter Paint the Sky

In the morning light, we rise,
With giggles dancing, hearts so free.
A symphony of joyous sighs,
Laughter painting all we see.

Colors swirl in bright delight,
As clouds become our canvas wide.
Each chuckle twinkling, pure and bright,
Our spirits soar, the world our ride.

The gentle breeze joins in the song,
Whispers of joy that never cease.
Together we feel we belong,
In laughter's warmth, we find our peace.

As sunlight fades, stars start to peek,
We gather 'round for tales and cheer.
In every laugh, there's love we seek,
Uniting us, our bonds hold dear.

Letting laughter weave the night,
With dreams and smiles, our hearts take flight.
Laughter echoes, pure and bold,
A story of joy forever told.

Dreams Unfolding Like Petals

In the garden where dreams grow,
Whispers of hope, so soft, so sweet.
Each petal opens, bright with glow,
    A symbol of a life complete.

Beneath the sky, so vast and wide,
Nature unfolds its precious grace.
In every bloom, a wish inside,
A promise wrapped in soft embrace.

Time drips slowly, moments sway,
Like petals dancing in the breeze.
With every dawn, a brand new day,
A chance to dream, to love, to breathe.

When shadows fall and doubts invade,
We close our eyes and find our way.
With courage, like a bloom displayed,
    We rise again, come what may.

Dreams like flowers, bright and bold,
    Unfolding stories yet untold.
In the garden of our heart's desires,
We cultivate our soul's true fires.

Radiant Skies of Uncharted Possibilities

Beneath the heavens, vast and blue,
We gaze at dreams that call our names.
With every glance, our spirits flew,
Exploring paths, igniting flames.

Clouds drift softly, whispers clear,
Each ray of light a path we find.
In every heartbeat, hope draws near,
Encouraging the open mind.

The stars remind us, pure and bright,
That dreams are not just for the night.
With every step, a spark ignites,
Creating waves of new delights.

We chase horizons, wild and far,
With courage, hearts begin to soar.
In limitless skies, our dreams ajar,
Unlocking realms of evermore.

Radiant skies call us to roam,
To chase the wonders, make them home.
In every heartbeat, possibilities gleam,
Encouraging us to chase a dream.

Kaleidoscope of Wishes in Flight

Wishes swirling in the air,
Each one a dream, a vibrant hue.
Floating softly, free as prayer,
Creating worlds both bright and new.

In a dance of colors bright,
Like butterflies, they chase the sun.
Each wish a spark, a pure delight,
A journey where our hearts can run.

Through the lens of life's embrace,
We see reflections of our dreams.
A kaleidoscope of endless grace,
Where hope is woven, light redeems.

As twilight sets the stars aglow,
Our wishes shimmer, wild and true.
In every heart, a fire we sow,
A flame that guides us, bright and blue.

Kaleidoscope of love and light,
We soar beyond, our dreams take flight.
In every moment, we will find,
A world of magic, soul entwined.

Embracing Tomorrow's Gentle Breeze

Whispers of hope in the air,
Softly they glide, beyond despair.
With each breath, a promise anew,
The dawn awakens, bright and true.

Golden rays kiss the earth's face,
Inviting all to join the race.
In stillness, dreams begin to rise,
Wrapped in warmth, beneath clear skies.

Leaves flutter, dance with delight,
Guided by currents, taking flight.
Nature's call, a gentle tease,
Embracing tomorrow's gentle breeze.

Moments linger, sweet and rare,
Every heartbeat, an answered prayer.
The world, a canvas vast and wide,
With tomorrow as our faithful guide.

So let us walk, hand in hand,
Through fields of joy, across the land.
United in this blissful spree,
Together we'll embrace the glee.

Awakening to the Dance of Delight

Morning light spills on the floor,
Inviting dreams from yesterday's door.
With every stretch, the world sings,
Awakening to what life brings.

Soft petals open, colors bloom,
Joy dances lightly, dispelling gloom.
A symphony of laughter starts,
Painting love in all our hearts.

Gentle breezes carry the tune,
As sunbeams waltz beneath the moon.
Time slips by in playful spins,
Our spirit lifts, adventure begins.

With every step, the earth feels bright,
The stars above, our guiding light.
We twirl and sway, lost in the night,
Awakening to the dance of delight.

Beneath the sky, we breathe in free,
Living life as it's meant to be.
In every glance, a world ignites,
Together we share these wondrous sights.

Echoes of Laughter in the Meadow

Across the fields where shadows play,
Echoes of laughter fill the day.
Children's voices blend with the breeze,
Joyful moments create memories.

Butterflies flit from flower to flower,
Nature blooms in this vibrant hour.
Sunbeams dance on the leaves so green,
Painting scenes of a life serene.

With every giggle, the world takes flight,
In the meadow, everything feels right.
Laughter rings as a sweet refrain,
Chasing away all hints of pain.

Kites soar high, painted with dreams,
Life unfolds, bursting at the seams.
In this space, we find our peace,
Echoes of laughter never cease.

As twilight wraps the day with grace,
Memories linger in this place.
Hearts unite in the twilight's glow,
Forever marked by the love we sow.

Celestial Visions of a Bright Tomorrow

Stars above shimmer like gems,
Casting hopes on all our dreams.
Celestial visions light the way,
Guiding hearts with gentle sway.

In quiet nights, we come alive,
With every wish, our spirits thrive.
The universe whispers its songs,
In this harmony, we belong.

Dreamers gather, eyes open wide,
With faith like ships, we sail the tide.
Together we paint the future bright,
With dreams ignited by starlit night.

Hands entwined, we walk through time,
Creating rhythms, a perfect rhyme.
Echoes of hope in every breath,
Defying darkness, conquering death.

As dawn breaks, the sky ignites,
Rich with colors of hopeful sights.
In each heartbeat, a promise glows,
Celestial visions as life flows.

A Symphony of Radiant Possibilities

In the dawn's first light, dreams unfold,
Whispers of hope in hues of gold.
Embrace the spark, let desires arise,
The world awaits beneath open skies.

Each heartbeat dances to a soft tune,
As stars farewell, blessing the moon.
With courage ignited, we'll take a stand,
Creating a future, together we'll land.

The canvas of life, in colors so bright,
Every journey begins with a flight.
With laughter and joy, we launch from the ground,
In this symphony, love knows no bounds.

Through valleys of doubt, we traverse so free,
Hand in hand, just you and me.
The symphony swelling, each note in its place,
As we weave our dreams in this sacred space.

Let the echoes ring, let our spirits soar,
In a realm of wonder, we'll seek even more.
With radiant possibilities lighting the way,
Together we'll conquer, come what may.

The Morning Star's Serenade

Under the heavens, a soft glow shines,
The morning star beckons, with tender signs.
Its melody dances on whispers of air,
Promising dreams, dispelling despair.

As dew-kissed petals greet the sun's embrace,
Nature awakens with gentle grace.
Each note a reminder of hope anew,
In the serenade, hearts find their true.

The tranquil symphony of rustling leaves,
In the sweet song, the soul believes.
With warmth surrounding, fears drift away,
In the morning light, we seize the day.

Birds take flight, soaring up high,
Painting the canvas of the endless sky.
The harmony wraps us, a soothing balm,
In the serenade's arms, we find our calm.

Together we rise, as the world starts to sing,
In this beautiful moment, joy we will bring.
The morning star whispers, a guiding light,
In its soft serenade, everything feels right.

Threads of Bliss Weaved in Daylight

Golden rays weave through the trees so tall,
Crafting a tapestry, a vibrant call.
Each thread a memory, stitched with care,
In the fabric of time, love lingers there.

Laughter cascades like a sparkling stream,
Coloring moments with a vivid dream.
We gather the threads, with hearts open wide,
In the daylight's embrace, we'll dance side by side.

As shadows dance softly, the sun starts to fade,
We cherish the warmth that the daylight made.
With every stitch, our stories align,
In this quilt of togetherness, destiny shines.

Through every season, the threads intertwine,
Binding our journeys, forever divine.
In blissful devotion, we find our way,
In the light of the sun, come what may.

So let us weave love with threads pure and bright,
In the daylight's glow, every fear takes flight.
For in this creation, our spirits will blend,
Threads of bliss woven, a bond without end.

Gentle Breezes of Euphoria

A whispering breeze drifts through the trees,
Bringing with it a tranquil tease.
With every sigh, the world feels light,
In the gentle currents, hearts take flight.

Awake to the dance of petals and leaves,
In this sweet moment, the spirit believes.
Barefoot on grass, we twirl and sway,
Together we greet the break of day.

In laughter and joy, we feel the embrace,
Fleeting like shadows, yet leaving a trace.
As sunbeams shimmer on water's face,
The breezes of euphoria find their place.

With every heartbeat, we find new heights,
In the soft glow of the magical lights.
Together we wander, lost in the bliss,
In gentle breezes, we find our kiss.

So let us explore under skies so clear,
With love as our guide, we shed every fear.
In the warmth of the sun, we'll forever roam,
Gentle breezes of euphoria lead us home.

Illuminated Paths Beneath a Smiling Sky

Footsteps trace the golden light,
Where shadows dance in pure delight.
Each moment shines, a fleeting gift,
A whispering breeze, the spirit's lift.

Beneath the sky, so vast and wide,
We wander forth, our hearts our guide.
With every step, new worlds appear,
A symphony for all to hear.

Through tangled woods and meadows bright,
The sunbeams laugh, embracing night.
The paths we choose, both near and far,
Illuminate our hidden star.

In harmony, the cosmos sways,
Each breath we take, a dance, a phrase.
The trail ahead, it calls us near,
With every heartbeat, love is clear.

Let us remember, soft and sweet,
The joy in every step, our feet.
For in this life, so rich, alive,
We find the strength in love to thrive.

Waves of Color

Crimson blush upon the sea,
Whispers of joy, wild and free.
Each ripple tells a tale untold,
In a canvas bright, bold and gold.

Azure skies cradle the light,
As waves crash in pure delight.
Luminous dreams surf the crest,
In this moment, we find rest.

Violet hues, like secrets spun,
Embrace the twilight, day is done.
Patterns swirl in ebb and flow,
A dance of color, ever aglow.

Emerald whispers kiss the shore,
In every wave, we find rapport.
Together, we weave tales anew,
In a tapestry of every hue.

With sunsets glowing, hearts unite,
In waves of color, pure delight.
The ocean's song, forever sweet,
Draws us close, our souls repeat.

Dancing in Daybreak

As dawn unfolds, the shadows flee,
Painting skies in harmony.
Golden rays touch every leaf,
In this dance, we find belief.

Twinkles shimmer on the dew,
Nature sings with every hue.
A melody of sweet rebirth,
As light awakens all the earth.

We twirl beneath the waking skies,
With hearts like birds, we learn to rise.
In every glance, a spark ignites,
In daybreak's glow, our spirit lights.

Every breath, a gift we share,
In the stillness, we are rare.
With open arms, we greet the morn,
In love's embrace, our dreams are born.

Together, we will chase the light,
In this rhythm, feel the flight.
Daybreak's dance, forever sought,
In this moment, love is caught.

Serenity in Sunrise

Softly glows the morning sun,
Whispers of a day begun.
In stillness found, a gentle sigh,
As dreams dissolve in the sky.

The world awakens, calm and bright,
With every hue, a pure delight.
A moment's peace, a sacred space,
In the light, we find our place.

Birdsong drifts on tender breeze,
Embracing hearts with tranquil ease.
In harmony, the day unfolds,
A promise wrapped in warmth and gold.

Golden rays dance on the lake,
In this stillness, souls awake.
Holding hands, we share this view,
A sunrise born anew, anew.

Let worries fade, the past dissolve,
In each moment, we evolve.
With open hearts, we rise and shine,
In serenity, our spirits intertwine.